Floral Alphabet Coloring Book

Leslie Tillett

Dover Publications, Inc.
New York

Publisher's Note

From A to Z, the alphabet in this book presents an amazing variety of floral life (using this term in the broadest sense to include all members of the vegetable kingdom). The name of each flower, fruit, vegetable, plant or mushroom begins with the letter within which it appears. Test yourself—see how many you can identify before you check the answers in the key beginning on page 27. For added enjoyment, the letters together with the images inside them may be colored in any way you feel is suitable. Samples of colored-in letters are shown on the covers.

Floral Alphabet Coloring Book is a new work,
first published by Dover Publications, Inc., in 1987.

International Standard Book Number: 0-486-25511-5

Manufactured in the United States of America
Dover Publications, Inc., 31 East 2nd Street, Mineola, N.Y. 11501

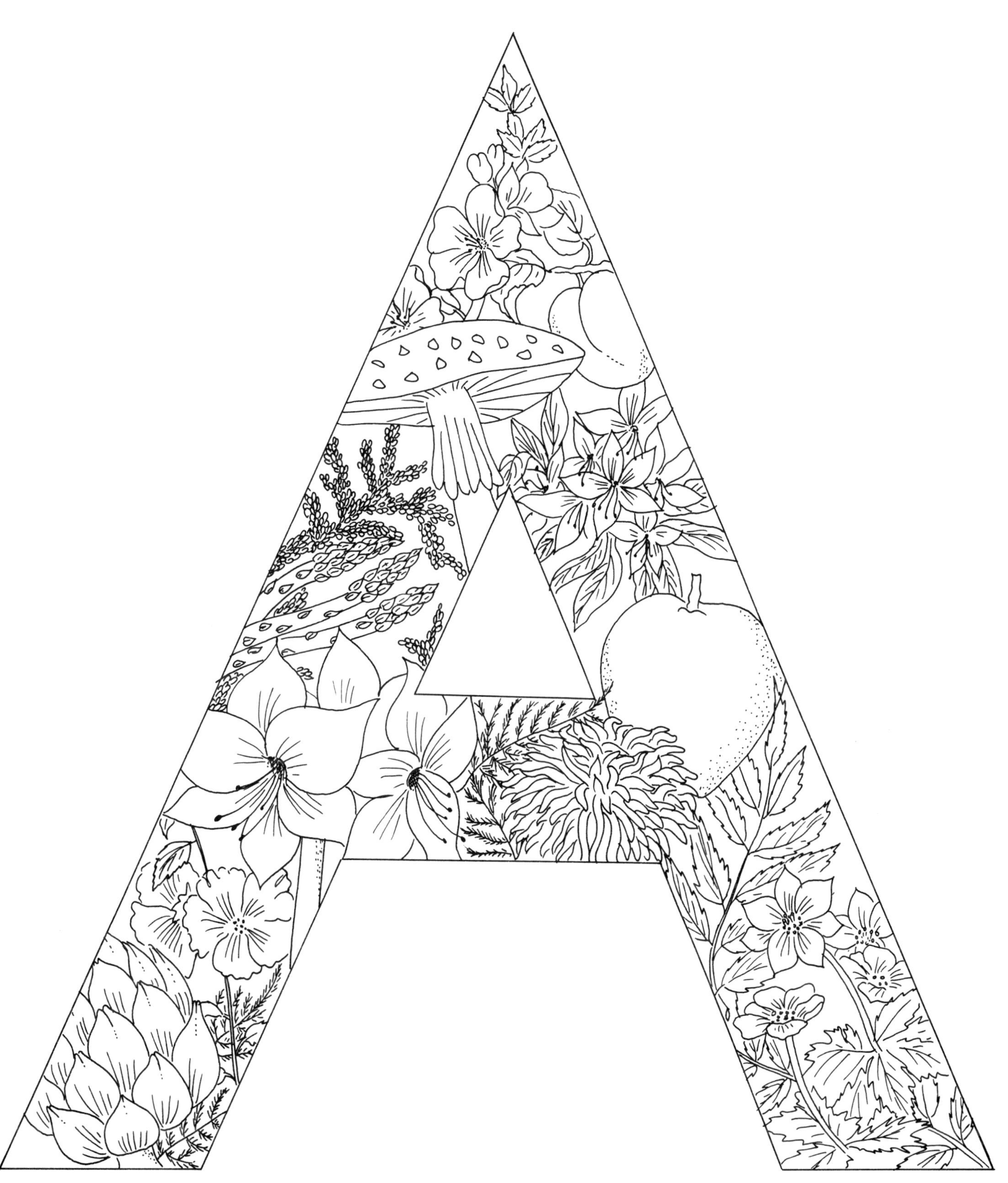

Key to Plants

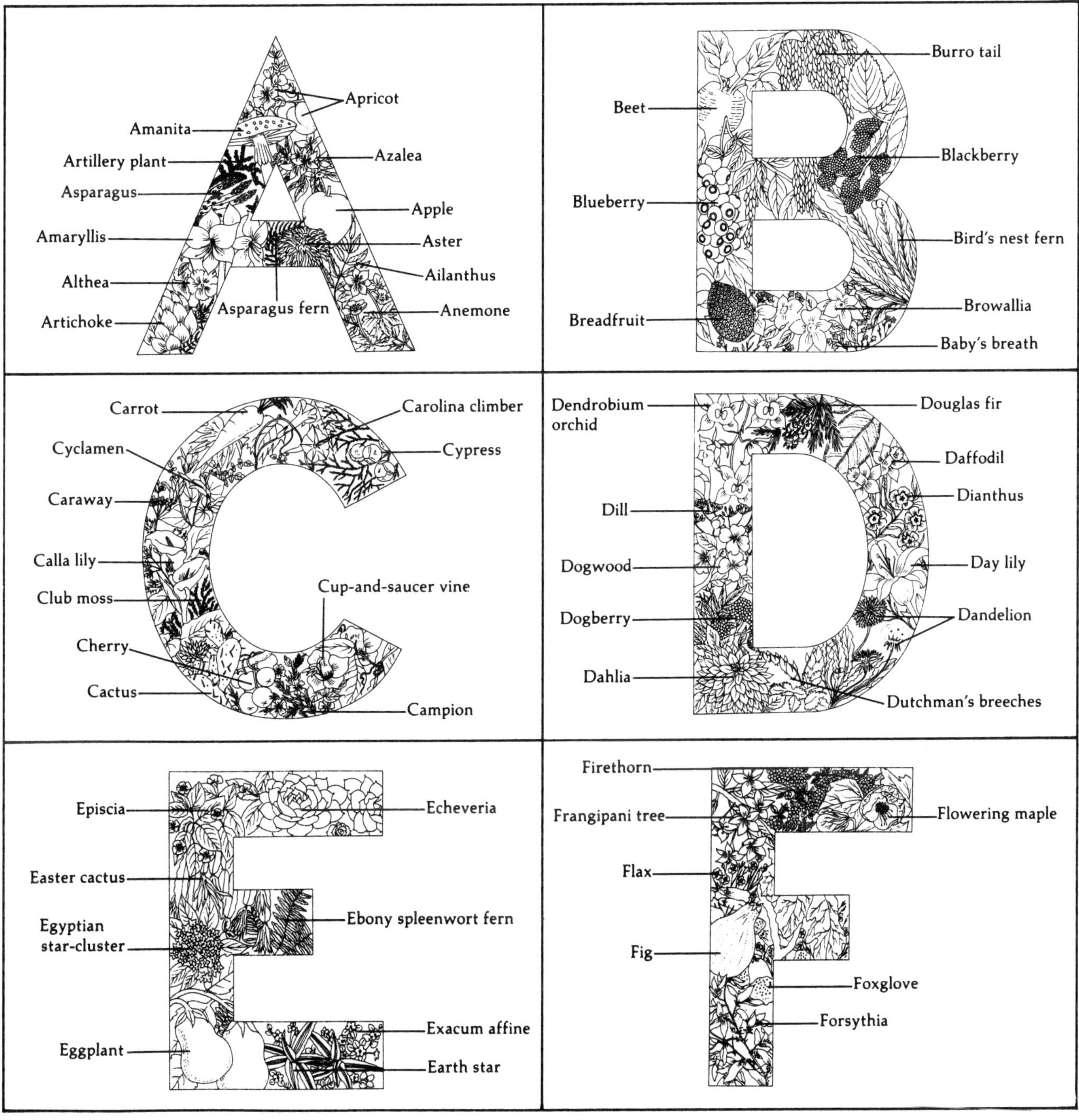
Apricot
Amanita
Artillery plant
Azalea
Asparagus
Apple
Amaryllis
Aster
Ailanthus
Althea
Asparagus fern
Anemone
Artichoke
Burro tail
Beet
Blackberry
Blueberry
Bird's nest fern
Breadfruit
Browallia
Baby's breath
Carrot
Carolina climber
Cyclamen
Cypress
Caraway
Calla lily
Club moss
Cup-and-saucer vine
Cherry
Cactus
Campion
Dendrobium orchid
Douglas fir
Daffodil
Dianthus
Dill
Dogwood
Day lily
Dogberry
Dandelion
Dahlia
Dutchman's breeches
Episcia
Echeveria
Easter cactus
Ebony spleenwort fern
Egyptian star-cluster
Exacum affine
Eggplant
Earth star
Firethorn
Frangipani tree
Flowering maple
Flax
Fig
Foxglove
Forsythia

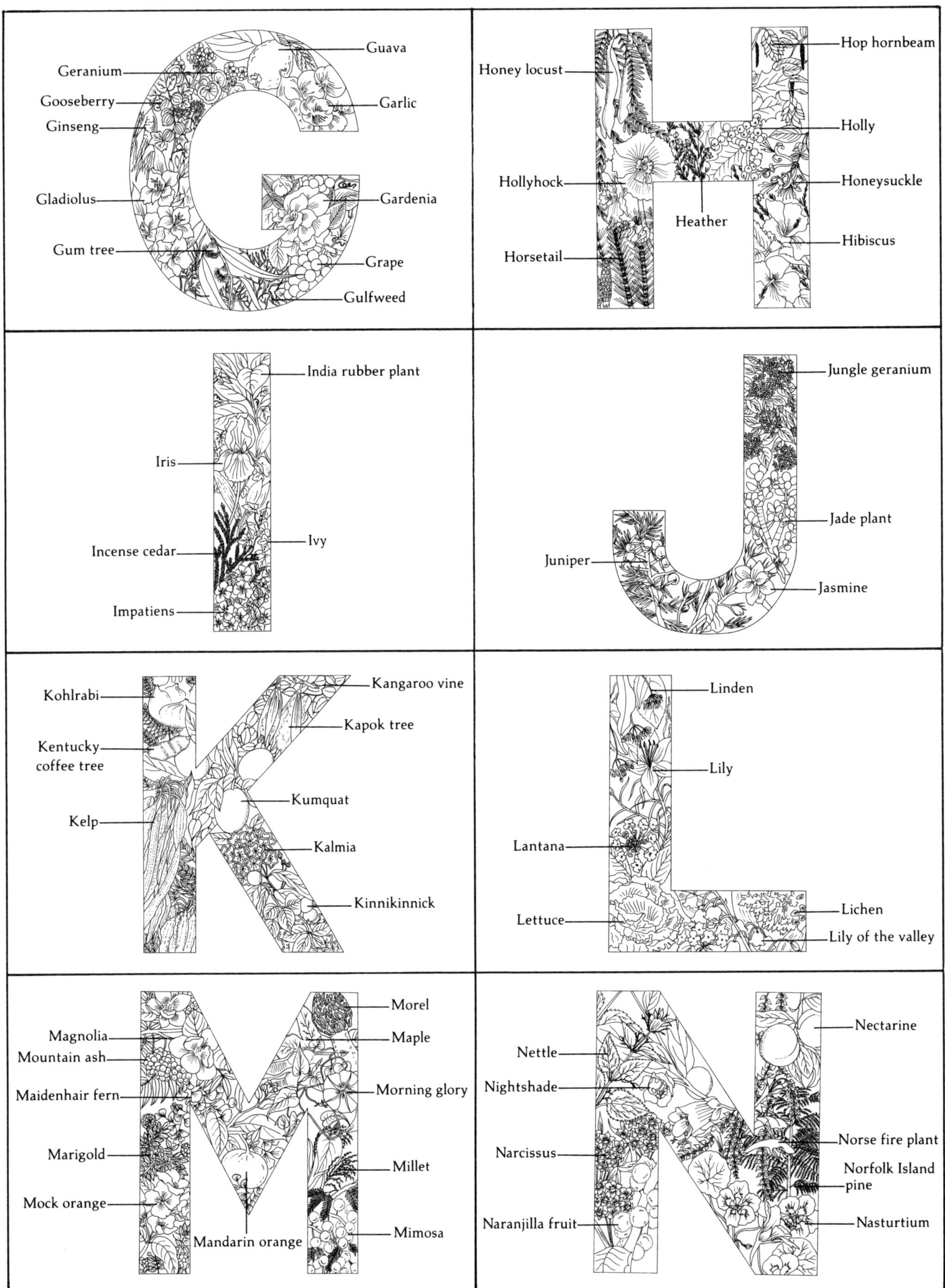
Guava
Geranium
Gooseberry
Garlic
Ginseng
Gladiolus
Gardenia
Gum tree
Grape
Gulfweed
Hop hornbeam
Honey locust
Holly
Hollyhock
Honeysuckle
Heather
Hibiscus
Horsetail
India rubber plant
Iris
Ivy
Incense cedar
Impatiens
Jungle geranium
Jade plant
Juniper
Jasmine
Kangaroo vine
Kohlrabi
Kapok tree
Kentucky coffee tree
Kumquat
Kelp
Kalmia
Kinnikinnick
Linden
Lily
Lantana
Lichen
Lettuce
Lily of the valley
Morel
Magnolia
Maple
Mountain ash
Maidenhair fern
Morning glory
Marigold
Millet
Mock orange
Mimosa
Mandarin orange
Nectarine
Nettle
Nightshade
Norse fire plant
Narcissus
Norfolk Island pine
Nasturtium
Naranjilla fruit

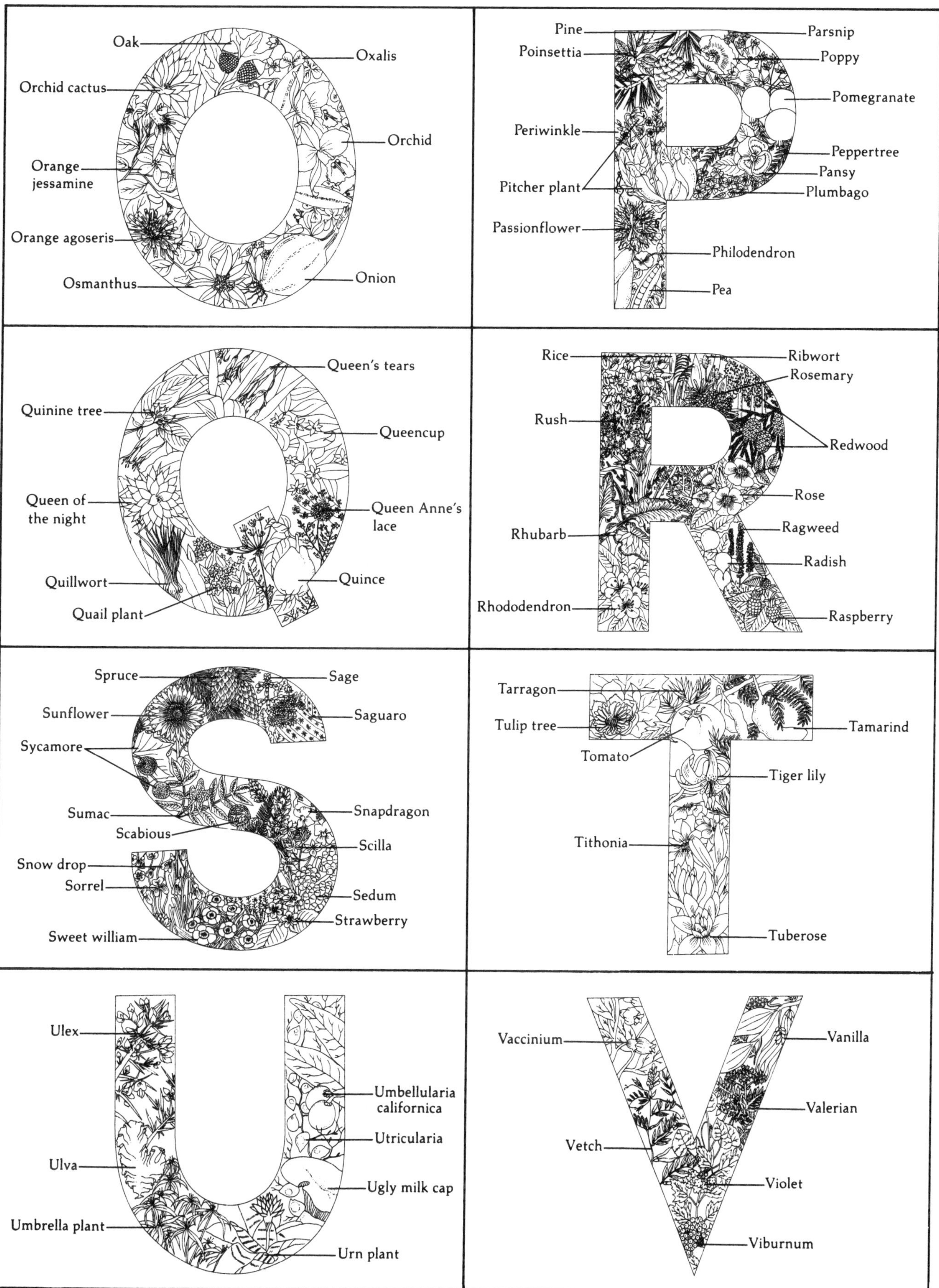
Oak
Oxalis
Orchid cactus
Orchid
Orange jessamine
Orange agoseris
Osmanthus
Onion
Pine
Parsnip
Poinsettia
Poppy
Pomegranate
Periwinkle
Peppertree
Pansy
Pitcher plant
Plumbago
Passionflower
Philodendron
Pea
Queen's tears
Quinine tree
Queencup
Queen of the night
Queen Anne's lace
Quillwort
Quince
Quail plant
Rice
Ribwort
Rosemary
Rush
Redwood
Rose
Rhubarb
Ragweed
Radish
Rhododendron
Raspberry
Spruce
Sage
Sunflower
Saguaro
Sycamore
Sumac
Snapdragon
Scabious
Scilla
Snow drop
Sorrel
Sedum
Strawberry
Sweet william
Tarragon
Tulip tree
Tamarind
Tomato
Tiger lily
Tithonia
Tuberose
Ulex
Umbellularia californica
Utricularia
Ulva
Ugly milk cap
Umbrella plant
Urn plant
Vaccinium
Vanilla
Valerian
Vetch
Violet
Viburnum

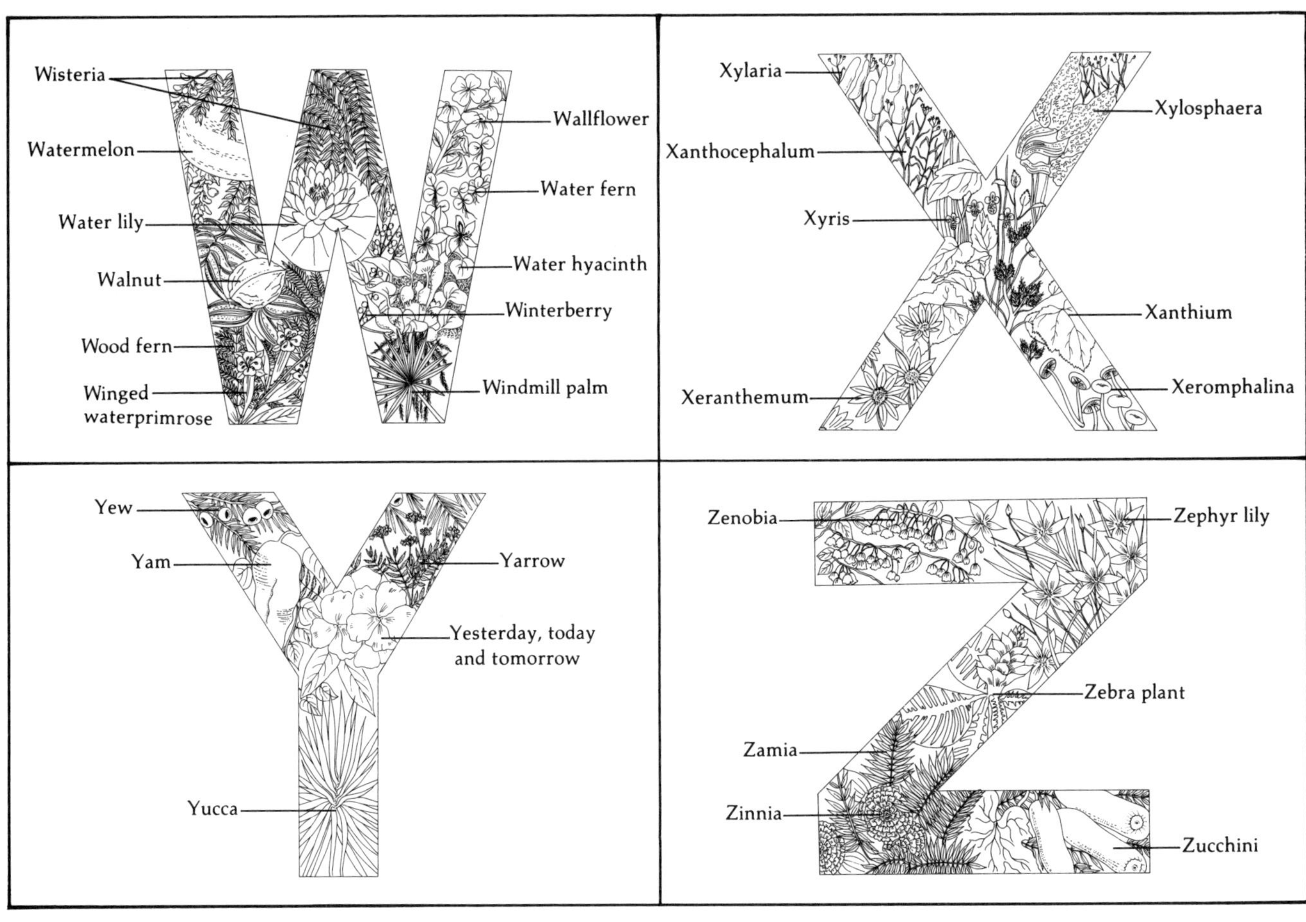
Wisteria
Watermelon
Water lily
Walnut
Wood fern
Winged waterprimrose
Wallflower
Water fern
Water hyacinth
Winterberry
Windmill palm
Xylaria
Xanthocephalum
Xyris
Xeranthemum
Xylosphaera
Xanthium
Xeromphalina
Yew
Yam
Yucca
Yarrow
Yesterday, today and tomorrow
Zenobia
Zamia
Zinnia
Zephyr lily
Zebra plant
Zucchini